FRAMEWORKS FOR
HIGHER
EDUCATION
IN
HOMELAND
SECURITY

Committee on Educational Paradigms for Homeland Security

Policy and Global Affairs

NATIONAL RESEARCH COUNCIL
OF THE NATIONAL ACADEMIES

THE NATIONAL ACADEMIES PRESS
Washington, D.C.
www.nap.edu

THE NATIONAL ACADEMIES PRESS   500 Fifth Street, N.W.   Washington, DC 20001

NOTICE: The project that is the subject of this report was approved by the Governing Board of the National Research Council, whose members are drawn from the councils of the National Academy of Sciences, the National Academy of Engineering, and the Institute of Medicine. The members of the committee responsible for the report were chosen for their special competences and with regard for appropriate balance.

This study was supported by Grant No. N00014-05-1-0011 between the National Academies and the Department of Homeland Security, as administered through the Office of Naval Research. The views presented in this report are those of the National Research Council Committee on Educational Paradigms for Homeland Security and are not necessarily those of the funding agencies.

International Standard Book Number 0-309-09295-7

Additional copies of this report are available from the National Academies Press, 500 Fifth Street, N.W., Lockbox 285, Washington, DC 20055; (800) 624-6242 or (202) 334-3313 (in the Washington metropolitan area); Internet, http://www.nap.edu.

THE NATIONAL ACADEMIES
Advisers to the Nation on Science, Engineering, and Medicine

The **National Academy of Sciences** is a private, nonprofit, self-perpetuating society of distinguished scholars engaged in scientific and engineering research, dedicated to the furtherance of science and technology and to their use for the general welfare. Upon the authority of the charter granted to it by the Congress in 1863, the Academy has a mandate that requires it to advise the federal government on scientific and technical matters. Dr. Ralph J. Cicerone is president of the National Academy of Sciences.

The **National Academy of Engineering** was established in 1964, under the charter of the National Academy of Sciences, as a parallel organization of outstanding engineers. It is autonomous in its administration and in the selection of its members, sharing with the National Academy of Sciences the responsibility for advising the federal government. The National Academy of Engineering also sponsors engineering programs aimed at meeting national needs, encourages education and research, and recognizes the superior achievements of engineers. Dr. Wm. A. Wulf is president of the National Academy of Engineering.

The **Institute of Medicine** was established in 1970 by the National Academy of Sciences to secure the services of eminent members of appropriate professions in the examination of policy matters pertaining to the health of the public. The Institute acts under the responsibility given to the National Academy of Sciences by its congressional charter to be an adviser to the federal government and, upon its own initiative, to identify issues of medical care, research, and education. Dr. Harvey V. Fineberg is president of the Institute of Medicine.

The **National Research Council** was organized by the National Academy of Sciences in 1916 to associate the broad community of science and technology with the Academy's purposes of furthering knowledge and advising the federal government. Functioning in accordance with general policies determined by the Academy, the Council has become the principal operating agency of both the National Academy of Sciences and the National Academy of Engineering in providing services to the government, the public, and the scientific and engineering communities. The Council is administered jointly by both Academies and the Institute of Medicine. Dr. Ralph J. Cicerone and Dr. Wm. A. Wulf are chair and vice chair, respectively, of the National Research Council.

www.national-academies.org

COMMITTEE ON EDUCATIONAL PARADIGMS FOR HOMELAND SECURITY

Irwin Feller (*Chair*), Senior Visiting Scientist, American Association for the Advancement of Science (AAAS)
Johnnie Carson, Senior Vice President, National Defense University
Max M. Houck, Director, Forensic Science Initiative, West Virginia University
Heather Kiriakou, Intelligence Fellow, Council on Foreign Relations
Arie W. Kruglanski, Distinguished Professor of Psychology, University of Maryland
Monica Schoch-Spana, Senior Fellow, University of Pittsburgh Medical Center (UPMC) Center for Biosecurity
Debra Stewart, President, Council of Graduate Schools

Principal Project Staff

Merrilea Mayo, Director, Government-University-Industry Research Roundtable
Yvette White, Senior Research Associate, Government-University-Industry Research Roundtable
Denise Greene, Administrative Coordinator, Government-University-Industry Research Roundtable
Hsiu-Ming Saunders, Intern, Government-University-Industry Research Roundtable

Acknowledgments

This report has been reviewed in draft form by individuals chosen for their diverse perspective and technical expertise, in accordance with procedures approved by the National Academies Report Review Committee. The purpose of this independent review is to provide candid and critical comments that will assist the institution in making its published report as sound as possible and to ensure that the report meets institutional standards for objectivity, evidence, and responsiveness to the committee charge. The review comments and draft manuscript remain confidential to protect the integrity of the process.

We wish to thank the following individuals for their review of this report: Lewis Branscomb, Harvard University; Gilbert Merkx, Duke University; Greg Moser, University of Denver; Thomas Schelling, University of Maryland; John Steinbruner, University of Maryland; and Thomas Terndrup, University of Alabama, Birmingham.

Although the reviewers listed above provided constructive comments and suggestions, they were not asked to endorse the conclusions or recommendations, nor did they see the final draft of the report before its release. The review of this report was overseen by John Bailar, University of Chicago. Appointed by the National Research Council, he was responsible for making certain that an independent examination of this report was carried out in accordance with institutional procedures and that all review comments were carefully considered. Responsibility for the final content of the report rests entirely with the authoring committee and the institution.

The following corrections are contained in this revised version of the original report: on page 9, the Coast Guard was removed from the listing of homeland security-related career opportunities. The Coast Guard is part of the Department of Homeland Security and should not be singled out as a standalone entity. On page 20, the number of fellowships provided by the Department of Homeland Security was overstated. The correct number of fellowships currently offered is 50.

Contents

Introduction   1

What Is Homeland Security?   3

What Is the Role of the Higher Education Community in
Homeland Security?   5

Parallels Between Homeland Security and
Area Studies, International Relations, and Science Policy   9

Current and Proposed Educational Programs in
Homeland Security   15

Summary   23

Appendixes

A   Committee Member Biographies   25

B   Workshop Agenda   31

C   Workshop Speaker Biographies   35

D   Workshop Participants   41

E   Sample Organizations Offering Homeland Security
Education Programs   45

Introduction

After the terrorist attacks on September 11, 2001, the U.S. academic community responded with an outpouring of course offerings, concentrations, certificates, and degree programs for students wishing to further their knowledge of "homeland security." Such initiatives, both informal and more formalized ones, incorporated inquiries into a wide range of topics, from the root causes of the violent act, to appropriate government policies for confronting this kind of danger, to more practical training for professional responders. The format of the response ranged from "teach-ins" to first responders' training to master's degree programs. The manifestation of interest was a "thousand flowers blooming," without apparent guidance, direction, or input at the national level.

To consider what, if any, national imperatives should drive such course offerings and programs—particularly in higher education—the National Academies' Policy and Global Affairs Division convened a committee, with the sponsorship of the Department of Homeland Security (DHS)'s Office of University Programs. The charge given to the committee was to

- discuss whether there are core pedagogical and skill-based homeland security program needs;
- examine current and proposed education programs focusing on various aspects of homeland security;
- comment on the possible parallels between homeland security, area studies, international relations, and science policy, as developed or emerging academic thrusts; and

- suggest potential curricula needs, particularly those that involve interdisciplinary aspects.

In further clarification from the sponsor, the committee was asked to focus on programs in higher education and specifically not to examine first responder or community training activities by colleges and universities—not for lack of importance, but because these types of activities were sufficiently prominent and pervasive that they were already under separate examination by DHS. Also excluded from consideration were the plethora of academic research activities and research programs related to homeland security needs, which were the subject of a prior study.[1] As a result of these intentional omissions, the present study concentrated almost exclusively on coursework-related offerings, primarily at the undergraduate and graduate levels.

The committee was aided in its deliberations by the content of a workshop held on April 26, 2004. The workshop included both plenary presentations and breakout sessions designed to address key questions in homeland security education (see Appendix B). In addition, the committee generated an illustrative list of academic programs in homeland security (as distinct from research programs), with the understanding that a more exhaustive list of such programs was simultaneously being compiled by the Homeland Security Institute (HSI). Because the HSI list of programs was not publicly available as of the writing of this report, we have included the working list used by the committee as Appendix E.

A handful of committee meetings and a single workshop by no means exhaust the topic at hand. For this reason, the present report does not offer a definitive set of formal findings and recommendations. Nonetheless, the committee is pleased to offer the following preliminary analysis of educational issues in homeland security. This report is viewed as a "working" analysis to be subsequently examined, supplemented, and possibly modified through a more extensive and systematic exploration of the current array of educational offerings in the homeland security domain. During review, it was specifically pointed out that an analysis of educational programs promoted/offered by federal agencies outside DHS could provide helpful context. The committee itself also recognizes that the area of professional school offerings needs further development, as this topic was on the margins of the present endeavor. We leave these activities to future workshops and studies.

---

[1] Alan Shaw, "University Research Centers of Excellence for Homeland Security: A Summary Report of a Workshop," 2004, Washington, DC: The National Academies Press.

What Is Homeland Security?

Characteristic of early committee deliberations and of the workshop proceedings was the realization that no well-articulated, explicitly delineated, and widely shared definition of U.S. "homeland security" exists. The phrase itself came into being as a result of, and in concert with, the dissolution of the prevailing Cold War-era paradigm of U.S. national security, a catastrophic terrorist assault on U.S. soil, a major reorganization of government unprecedented since the 1947 National Security Act (which created the Department of Defense [DOD], the Central Intelligence Agency [CIA], and the National Security Council [NSC]), and the integration of 22 government agencies with widely disparate historic missions and work cultures into the current Department of Homeland Security.

To facilitate its charge, the committee adopted the following as its working definition: "Any area of inquiry whose improved understanding could make U.S. peoples safer from extreme, unanticipated threats." Two strong, divergent opinions characterized further attempts to refine the definition and were equally represented in workshop discussion: (1) "homeland security" includes those threats that are man-made in origin (the exclusive view) or (2) "homeland security" includes man-made, technological, and natural threats (the inclusive view). The difference in the two definitions lies in the area of protection from natural or technological disasters. This area is—for better or worse—already well defined academically. As pointed out by Dr. Wayne Blanchard of FEMA, emergency management curricula across the nation have have been tracked, shared, standardized, and refined via university interaction with FEMA's Emergency Management Institute for over 10 years, with many institutions sharing exactly the same syllabi, course notes, and "prevention-preparedness-re-sponse-recovery" paradigm.[1] For the practical purposes of this report, vir-tually all the conclusions herein apply equally well to both the inclusive and the exclusive views of homeland security. However, much of the de-scriptive text and Appendix E concentrate on the area which is less well defined academically, that of human-origin threats.

The committee faced the dilemma of having to evaluate education frameworks in homeland security *as if* a consensus on the term exists within government and the academy, when it does not. A priority for higher education should be to promote public and professional dialogue as to what constitutes a socially acceptable definition of homeland secu-rity and what are the practical institutional means to achieve it.

It is important to understand that, while the term "homeland secu-rity" arose out of specific historical/political events, its treatment in academia does not have, and does not need to have, a one-to-one corre-spondence to these events or to existing political structures. Most impor-tantly, the content of academic programs (see Appendix E) far exceeds the political and operational boundaries of the Department of Homeland Se-curity. The academic programs span areas such as public health, military history, international diplomacy, the psychological-sociological examina-tions of other cultures, and comparative government systems—areas not in the explicit domain of the department. Indeed, the academic context of homeland security could be stretched to include almost every discipline and topic area imaginable, with "homeland security" serving more as a target for the application of such studies, rather than as a descriptor of the studies themselves.

A multidisciplinary, multifaceted approach to homeland security edu-cation has substantial potential. For one, it can bridge the conceptual di-vides that currently plague our nation's security apparatus—for example, the division between domestic (law enforcement) and international (mili-tary) security, or between domestic (FBI) and foreign (CIA) intelligence, or between preexisting operations (FEMA, Office for Domestic Prepared-ness/Department of Justice) now trying to adapt to each other under the same agency roof (DHS). In academia, the turf can be replanted. Academic inquiry is not constrained by any particular agency's mission, configura-tion, or programmatic concerns.

---

[1]See *http://www.training.fema.gov/emiweb/edu/index.asp* for more information.

What Is the Role of the Higher Education Community in Homeland Security?

The appropriate role of colleges and universities in support of homeland security is rooted in the traditional strengths of America's higher education sector. Workshop participants agreed that these roles should include the following:

1. *Access to homeland security careers for students.* In service to students, the higher education sector should provide an educational path that would permit entry into a career supporting the goals of homeland security, whether in public, private, or nongovernmental (NGO) sectors.

2. *Relevant content knowledge, both specialized and generalized, for those who need it.* In service to the broad community, including concerned citizens, trained specialists, public officials, and the press, the higher education sector should be able to provide factual content concerning homeland security issues that is appropriate to the knowledge needs of the recipient.

3. *More informed citizens.* In service to the people of the United States, higher education should educate citizens who are knowledgeable about the nature of threats, both new and old, and about core democratic values that should be considered in devising principles, policies, and practices for confronting these threats.

4. *A forum for public debate.* In support of the democracy in which we live, the higher education sector should serve as one of the fora for public debate and decision on critical issues of the day.

The role of higher education in preparing students for homeland security-related careers was the major focus of the workshop presentations and hence of the sections that follow in this report. There was little substantive dialogue on how the university community might serve nonstudent specialists and the broader public (role numbers two and three). In part this was because community and first responder training were intentionally omitted from the scope of the workshop (see Introduction).

Workshop and committee deliberations often gravitated to vibrant discussions on the need for universities to sponsor public debate (role number four). The outpouring of enthusiasm for public debate seemed to be motivated by specific homeland security regulations that had recently and directly impacted academia. These same issues also had larger public policy dimensions, as workshop participants were quick to point out.

For example, Dr. Susan Cutter discussed the recent denial of public access to geographic data as an example of the trade-offs required when deciding to keep threat-relevant information exclusively within the governmental domain, subject to classification policies, versus sharing that information with the public and with the many private and nonprofit organizations and individuals that need measurement, intelligence, and historical data to prepare predictive models, reinforce infrastructure, design personnel screening systems, and so forth. When facing conventional war, U.S. policy makers and the public have generally viewed security threats as existing elsewhere, limited to the concerns of the U.S. military and national security experts. The 9/11 tragedy and the possibility of additional terrorist attacks on U.S. soil, however, necessarily undermine these conceptual and institutional boundaries. The civilian sector is now directly responsible for security matters, more so than at any time in recent U.S. history, for many reasons. Members of the public have an interest in personal protective measures for themselves and their families. Firefighters, police, emergency medical technicians, public health officials, urban planners, engineers, architects, and health care workers now have to manage novel threats to public safety and health, such as anthrax attacks and airplane-building collisions. All of these individuals need access to information on security threats to improve security within their own sphere of influence. Yet the nation does not have adequate institutional processes or paradigms for sharing that information.

Workshop participants and the committee viewed denial of public access to information as a measure that itself presented a significant security threat, particularly over the long term. Within higher education, the primary impact was to limit the system's ability to deliver individuals trained in the very areas required to deliver domestic safety and security.

For example, stringent government regulations on "select agent" research at universities, as well as the highly publicized indictment of plague researcher Thomas Butler, had inadvertently created disincentives for researchers to engage in work beneficial to U.S. defense against biological weapons.[1-4] Tighter visa restrictions and government contract restrictions had curtailed the participation of foreign students and faculty in research and learning at U.S. universities.[5,6] This trend, over the long run, may impede scientific and technological advances that support the U.S. economy, as well as preclude the positive influence of these visitors on their home countries' perception of, and relations with, the United States.[7-10] Controls over the publication of sensitive but unclassified research could further curtail researchers' interest and willingness to pursue work supportive of security goals.[11-16]

Another issue ripe for public debate emerged in workshop breakout sessions: the broad and often self-destructive social reaction to terrorist provocation. The immediate impact of an attack may be limited in scope,

---

[1] American Association of University Professors (AAUP), 2003, "Academic Freedom and National Security in a Time of Crisis," *Academe* 89:34-58.

[2] AAAS Issue Brief, "Science and National Security in the Post-9/11 Environment," *http://www.aaas.org/spp/post911/agents/index.shtml.*

[3] National Research Council (NRC), *Biotechnology Research in an Age of Terrorism*, 2004, Washington, DC: The National Academies Press.

[4] Letter, from National Academy of Sciences President Bruce Alberts and Institute of Medicine President Harvey Fineberg to Attorney General John Ashcroft, August 15, 2003, *http://www.fas.org/sgp/news/2003/08/nas081503.pdf.*

[5] Peter D. Syverson and Heath A. Brown, "Graduate Enrollment and Degrees 1986 to 2002," 2003, Washington, DC: Council of Graduate Schools (*http://www.cgsnet.org/pdf/GED%202002.pdf*).

[6] Heath A. Brown and Peter D. Syverson, "Findings from U.S. Graduate Schools on International Graduate Student Admission Trends," 2004, Washington, DC: Council of Graduate Schools (*http://www.cgsnet.org/pdf/Sept04FinalIntlAdmissionsSurveyReport.pdf*).

[7] AAUP, op. cit.

[8] AAAS, op. cit., *http://www.aaas.org/spp/post911/visas/.*

[9] Association of America Universities (AAU) and the Council on Governmental Relations (COGR), "Restrictions on Research Awards: Troublesome Clauses," *http://aau.edu/research/Rpt4.8.04.pdf.*

[10] National Science Board, "Science and Engineering (S&E) Indicators 2004," *http://www.nsf.gov/sbe/seind04/.*

[11] AAUP, op. cit.

[12] NRC, op. cit.

[13] AAAS, op. cit., *http://www.aaas.org/spp/post911/sbu/.*

[14] AAU and CGR, op. cit.

[15] Congressional Research Service Report RL31845, 2003, "Sensitive but Unclassified and Other Federal Security Controls on Scientific and Technical Information: History and Current Controversy."

[16] Congressional Research Service Report RL31695, 2004, "Balancing Scientific Publication and National Security Concerns: Issues for Congress."

but subsequent reactions by authorities or the larger population can amplify the event's detrimental effects. An attack by a Muslim leads to suspicion of all Muslims; an attack on an aircraft leads to broad refusal by travelers to fly (despite the fact that trains and buses are at least equally vulnerable), and so on. In 2001-2002 these two examples alone led, respectively, to violation of the rights of Muslim American citizens and severe financial depression of the airline industry—surely not desirable outcomes.

A complementary issue for collective consideration was the potential for security concerns to overshadow and "crowd out" alternative national imperatives, even those the "security" was intended to protect. Recent psychological research suggests that focusing strongly on a given objective pulls attention away from other objectives.[17] This frees individuals and groups to pursue the focal objective without the constraints normally exercised by those alternative objectives. Thus, an unchecked emphasis on "security" can impinge on individual human rights and the very democratic way of life that is at stake: for example, the values of equality of persons and respect for other cultures. This, in turn, may further reduce the prospects of security in the long term by deepening the chasm between different ethnicities within the United States as well as between the United States and other nations. Ultimately, and perhaps paradoxically, neglect of the alternative concerns can lead to undermining collective security in the long term.

Because a strong focus on security issues may encourage the pursuit of security through means that infringe on institutional freedoms (as the university research examples above demonstrate) or individual freedoms (as the McCarthyism excesses in the 1950s demonstrate), or have other adverse consequences, the committee feels that better educating the public, students, legislators, and media to recognize these trade-offs and their short- and long-term implications will be a necessary component of homeland security education. This view moves the perception of security from the popular one of purely military, law enforcement and intelligence activities to one that includes political, economic, cultural, and informational contributions and consequences. The need for this correction was brought forth in the workshop numerous times, is seen here in the discussion of public debate, and will be seen later in the discussion of a core curriculum for homeland security.

---

[17]J.Y. Shah, R. Friedman, and A.W. Kruglanski, 2002, "Forgetting All Else: On the Antecedents and Consequences of Goal Shielding," *Journal of Personality and Social Psychology* 83:1261-1280.

Parallels Between Homeland Security and Area Studies, International Relations, and Science Policy

To provide further insight into possible roles for homeland security education, it is possible to draw lessons from the past. Just as educational programs in homeland security emerged in response to the events of September 11, educational programs in area studies flourished in response to the Cold War. Official authorization and funding were first provided by the National Defense Education Act of 1958 and continue under Title VI of the U.S. Code to this day. (A precursor effort to area studies programs, the U.S. Army Specialized Training Program, was initiated during World War II but discontinued after the war's end.) International studies began even earlier, before World War II.[1]

In both area studies and homeland security studies, the national educational response was to a perceived threat and a corresponding national need. In both cases, the subject matter of the new coursework drew from multiple disciplines. Also, in both cases, there was at least one identifiable federal agency whose recruiting needs would be well served by students graduating from the new programs. For area studies, the perceived federal customers were the Central Intelligence Agency (CIA), the Department of Defense (DOD), and the Department of State.[2] For the scientific programs launched around the same time (post-Sputnik), the National

---

[1] On the history of international studies as a discipline, see Robert A. McCaughey, 1984, *International Studies and Academic Enterprise: A Chapter in the Enclosure of American Learning*, New York: Columbia University Press.

[2] Ibid.

Aeronautics and Space Administration (NASA) was the main benefi-ciary.[3] For current homeland security programs, the perceived federal customer is primarily the Department of Homeland Security (DHS). This perception persists despite homeland security-related career opportuni-ties in the Departments of Energy, Agriculture, Transportation, Housing and Urban Development, Health and Human Services, Treasury, Defense, Justice, and Commerce; as well as opportunities in the Postal Service and the Internal Revenue Service; and despite numerous nonfederal opportu-nities in port/airport security, urban planning, city/regional governance, public health, and virtually all forms of engineering.

Evidence supporting the public perception of DHS as the primary customer can be seen in educational programs that specifically claim that they will train students to become "homeland security specialists"[4] and in university websites that reference solely the Department of Homeland Security in their introductory material[5] or provide direct links only to DHS, among all the federal agencies.[6]

At this point, the course offerings and programs in homeland security are still in their infancy, and it may yet be possible to apply some caution-ary lessons learned from the nation's experience with area studies. The primary concern voiced in the breakout session on area studies was that it is a mistake to link an educational program too strongly to a single federal agency.

The danger to programs appears to be that public or political percep-tions of the agency can transfer easily to the educational program in ques-tion, regardless of their factual basis. Examples in support of this view can be found in news commentaries, discussion boards, and written docu-ments on area studies programs. For example, the Chronicle of Education Colloquy Debate, "Tarnished as a Spy?,"[7] considers whether area studies scholars should boycott the National Security Education Program, which provides fellowships to students in area studies. The rationale in favor of the boycott is that the program is "tainted" by its funding source. Another example of the perceived conflation of agency objectives and an educa-tional program is the open letter distributed by Michigan State University to its undergraduates considering enrolling in the National Security Edu-

---

[3]AAAS, 2004, "Trends in Non-defense R&D by Function, FY 1953-2005," February, http://www.aaas.org/spp/rd/histda05.pdf.

[4]http://www.directoryofschools.com/Homeland-Security.htm.

[5] http://ptesrv.apl.jhu.edu/04_5_catalog/homeland.html.

[6]http://homelandsecurity.osu.edu.

[7]"Tarnished as a Spy?," The Chronicle of Higher Education, August 8, 2002. Colloquy Dis-cussion: http://chronicle.com/colloquy/2002/spy/.

cational Program (area studies fellowships). The letter states: "In areas where mistrust of the U.S. Government exists, there are concerns that scholars and students who accept the funds may be perceived as either current or future employees of U.S. Government security and intelligence agencies (i.e., CIA, NSC, Defense Intelligence Agency [DIA], etc.)."[8]

The actual extent to which area studies students are seen by their host countries today as anything other than area studies students is unknown, and "mistrust of the U.S. government" can readily be transferred to any American abroad, regardless of academic specialty. Yet, as shown by the quotation above, at least one university has the perception that in the case of area studies, the funding source is publicly identifiable with the student and with the academic program. Anecdotal evidence from at least one federal agency represented at the workshop was that the aura of "CIA, NSC, DIA" involvement in area studies limits enrollment by skewing the demographics of program applicants. The biasing of the applicant pool occurs in accordance with the uneven partitioning of political views according to gender, ethnicity, income, and other demographic factors.

At home, educational programs in area studies are also subject to evaluation on a political basis—specifically, whether they are overly sympathetic, or obstinately unresponsive, to the needs of their "affiliated" government agency. This debate on the "usefulness" of the area studies curriculum to political goals has emerged in congressional testimony on Title VI.[9] The consequence for the university is that the debate both puts federal funding for area studies programs at risk and calls into question the field's inherent academic legitimacy. Area studies is perhaps the only discipline to have Congress attempt to impose a mandatory external advisory committee upon it (HR 3077, in 2003).

More broadly, there is a long history of concern within academia about possible alliances between researchers and U.S. military and intelligence agencies, with documented negative effects. For example, some Latin Americanists from the United States have confronted lingering suspicions on the part of host countries due to Project Camelot, a U.S. Army-funded social research enterprise into the problem of counterinsurgency in Latin America in the 1960s.[10,11] Controversies within cultural anthro-

---

[8]*http://studyabroad.msu.edu/scholarships/nsep.html.*

[9]Testimonies of David Ward before the House Subcommittee on Labor, HHS and Education Appropriations, April 23, 2003, and Terry Hartle and Stanley Kurz before the House Subcommittee on Select Education, June 19, 2003.

[10]Irving Louis Horowitz, ed., 1967, *The Rise and Fall of Project Camelot: Studies in the Relationship Between Social Science and Practical Politics,* Cambridge: The M.I.T. Press.

[11] Carolyn Fluehr-Lobban, ed., 1991, *Ethics and the Profession of Anthropology,* Philadelphia: University of Pennsylvania Press.

pology over the professional ethics of intelligence gathering (World War I) and conducting counterinsurgency research (Thailand, against the backdrop of the Vietnam War) have threatened academic careers and created rifts within the discipline about government contract support of ethnographic research.[12,13]

Further examination of the literature by the committee showed, and participants in the area studies breakout session pointed out, that there is a cautionary lesson to be learned from the area studies experience. Many of the programs supporting area studies and its students are, in themselves, well constructed and well liked by participants. An example is the National Security Education Program, which gives scholarship funding in exchange for career service at one of the federal security-related agencies. The problem is not the program itself, but the cultivation of a few such programs to the point that they dominate the field's source of students and funding. The Department of Homeland Security will need to secure public support for education in homeland security without allying itself so closely to homeland security programs that the agency and the educational objectives become intertwined in the public perception. For this reason, it would be helpful for the mandate for such educational programs to be as broad as possible.

From a practical standpoint, this means that financial support for such programs should come from an array of sectors (private as well as public; perhaps even international) and an array of providers within each sector. Should DHS choose to provide financial support for new academic programs, its initiatives can be guided by principles articulated in the National Academies report *Evaluating Federal Research Programs:*

1. selection of performers by competitive merit review set against clearly stated program objectives and selection criteria;
2. systematized external assessments of project, performer, and program performance; and
3. systematic opportunities for recompetition for multiple-year awards.[14]

These principles have been found to provide for the most effective

---

[12] Ibid.

[13] Eric Wakin, 1992, *Anthropology Goes to War: Professional Ethics and Counterinsurgency in Thailand*, University of Wisconsin: Center for Southeast Asian Studies.

[14] COSEPUP (Committee on Science, Engineering, and Public Policy), 1999, *Evaluating Federal Research Programs: Research and the Government Performance and Results Act*, Washington, D.C.: National Academy Press.

use of the nation's investments in knowledge-creating undertakings, to ensure the continuing vitality of awardee performance, and to allow for the regularized introduction of new innovative programs and performers.[15]

Just as funding paradigms may affect educational paradigms, so too may communication paradigms. To obtain the broadest public support, the communicated expectations of the academic programs should be that they prepare future employees for a wide range of employment, across all sectors, in a broad array of locations and job titles. Considering the breadth of the definition of homeland security given earlier, this should not prove difficult.

As discussed above, homeland security shares similarities with area studies in its close relationship to a national security need. However in the half-century intervening between the establishment of area studies and the dawn of homeland security studies, the educational landscape has changed. New opportunities have arisen. For example, there is now the opportunity to educate workers and the public in preventing threats, not just responding to them. Workshop participants with backgrounds in hazards assessment indicated that this is possible because there is greater understanding of many natural and (to a lesser extent) human-initiated phenomena, leading to better predictive models and potentially better decision making now than in the past. Furthermore, universities have made great progress in establishing mechanisms for interdisciplinary work (centers, interdisciplinary degree programs, joint faculty appointments, etc.).[16] Many of these were not in place when area studies was established as a field of inquiry. Finally, to come full circle, some of the educational forays made by then-new interdisciplinary "fields" such as area studies, national security studies, and even bioengineering can now provide content to the evolving educational studies in homeland security.

---

[15]Ibid.

[16]DBASSE (Division of Behavioral and Social Sciences and Education), 2003, *Evaluating and Improving Undergraduate Teaching in Science, Technology, Engineering, and Math*, Washington, D.C.: The National Academies Press.

Current and Proposed Educational Programs in Homeland Security

CURRENT PROGRAMS

A sampling of current educational programs in homeland security is given in Appendix E. This list was generated by an Internet search of the words "education" (plus "master's," "Ph.D.," "certificate," "university," etc.) and "homeland security." It is a survey only and makes no distinction on the basis of curriculum, permanence, date of implementation, size, or other potential filtering parameters. In accordance with the charge to the committee, this listing does not include research programs or first responder training programs.

Yet the breadth of offerings is evident. There are certificates, continuing education modules, master's, and professional master's degrees being offered. There are traditional classroom experiences and on-line learning programs. There are opportunities in every geographic region in the continental United States and in institutions of widely varying size and mission (community colleges, four-year undergraduate institutions, doctorate granting institutions). The content ranges from efforts rooted in technical prevention to workforce skills development to social understanding. Many programs have capitalized on the existing strengths of the parent institution, repackaging existing coursework in innovative ways, germinating new courses from established research thrusts, or gathering existing faculty into new research centers that not only follow new research pursuits but also spin off new academic offerings.

Perhaps the most natural transition to "homeland security" coursework has occurred in existing national security studies programs, where the overall curriculum was simply updated post-9/11 to include more homeland security content within each course and a smattering of new course offerings. A classic example of this phenomenon is the 25-year-old Security Studies program at Georgetown University, which had to change neither name, nor administrative structure, nor building, nor graduation requirements, nor degree titles to incorporate the study of homeland security into the fabric of its educational program.

Yet, since academic strengths differ widely among institutions, and since homeland security is an extremely broad topic, there is seemingly no end to the variation among programs that have developed since 9/11. Indeed this proliferation occasioned the committee's present charge to begin the process of systematizing and organizing data on the diversity of educational offerings according to some coherent scheme.

PROPOSED FRAMEWORKS

Given the breadth encompassed by the term homeland security as defined earlier, it is appropriate that there be a wide range of educational experiences available. This view argues strongly against the creation of an all-definitive, all-encompassing "Homeland Security University," or the development of independent academic tracks for "homeland security specialists." That is not to say that academic content in homeland security is completely formless. An important observation and potential organizing principle is that nearly all aspects of homeland security gravitate toward the issue of complex threats and how to manage them. This was the overriding theme in the workshop presentations.

The core literature that contributes expertise to understanding and managing these threats, derived from workshop presentations, consists of the following:

1. *Risk management and analysis* (intended to provide educational background in managing responsible resource allocation in proportion to threat probability, estimated threat magnitude, and the likelihood of amelioration through corrective action).

2. *Systems integration and management* (intended to facilitate an understanding of ways of forging cooperative mechanisms among the variety of agencies addressing aspects of homeland security).

3. *Social, cultural, psychological, political, historical, and operational dynamics of threats* (the study, from social, natural science, and humanities perspectives of the issues related to the roots of terrorism, its dynamic, its evolution, and its application).

4. *Legal, political, and ethical issues in threat response* (intended to provide an understanding of the psychological reactions that drive decision making in crisis, and an expanded view of the consequences on institutions, structures, ethnic relations, individual freedoms—and even security itself—of decision trade-offs made under crisis in the past).

5. *Decision-making tools and processes for the management and resolution of complex problems* (may include exposure to such technical tools as data networks and data mining, but may also include nontechnical approaches such as forecasting/future studies and scenario planning).

In addition to the core material, there may be threat-specific curricular enhancements that derive from, and are taught within, the context of the major discipline of the student—e.g., sensors, target hardening, crowd control, public health, demographics, emergency planning. These will vary tremendously by major, but can easily be combined with the core elements to provide a competency in homeland security *from the vantage point of a specific discipline or disciplines.*

According to the points listed above, workshop participants acknowledged that homeland security is not a discipline—at least not yet and not in the traditional sense. Instead, it is an area to which many academic specialties can be applied, but one that requires a certain core knowledge in order for the application to occur intelligently. The core is therefore recommended for anyone planning a career in the myriad of federal, state, and local agencies, nonprofit organizations, and even for-profit service providers engaged in homeland security work. Given the consideration above, the definition of homeland security, and the lessons learned from area studies, the committee proposes the following educational opportunities as being well suited to the provision of homeland security content-specific knowledge to students.

AT THE COMMUNITY COLLEGE LEVEL: EXPOSURE TO THE CORE

Community college representatives pointed out that in addition to their well-known roles in providing first responder training, community skills development, and serving as a forum for public debate, community colleges can introduce students to some elements of the core curriculum described above. This will then prepare students for a more in-depth specialization at a four-year institution. Though community college students are 23 percent less likely to earn a four-year degree than those who begin their careers in four-year institutions, they comprise approximately one-third of the college-going public.[1,2] Community college students are there-fore a nonnegligible component of the U.S. education system.

Many community colleges are already on the path to offering some of the core elements described in the previous section. For example, the Corinthian Colleges, which were represented at the workshop, offer an associate degree in homeland security, which captures elements three and four in their "domestic and international terrorism" offerings and their "business and ethics for security specialists" offerings, respectively.

The relevance of the five listed core elements to homeland security can be seen from the fact that some community colleges have intuitively absorbed them, though not necessarily in the form of a formal curriculum leading to an associate degree. For example, Bucks County Community College, the Community College of Philadelphia, Camden County College, Delaware County Community College, and Drexel University have collaborated to provide courses that cover all the core elements listed, but the course format is that of one-day continuing education modules, de-signed for a target audience of first responders.[3]

Core element number four—legal, political, and ethical issues in threat response—was surprisingly prominent in community college curricula. It had, however, received added visibility in the community college sector from two summits convened by the Community College National Center for Community Engagement. The latest summit, held in February 2004, emphasized the role of community colleges in dealing with the conse-quences and aftermath of homeland security measures, not only through preparative coursework initiatives—teaching students about the trade-offs and consequences to be expected—but also by hosting public debates and discussions within communities and by initiating active volunteer outreach programs.[4]

[1]Ray L. Christie and Philo Hutcheson, 1993, "Net Effects of Institutional Type on Bacca-laureate Degree Attainment of Traditional Students," *Community College Review* (Fall). Com-munity college students are only 10% less likely to earn a baccalaureate than students at four-year institutions if data are controlled for demographic variables such as high school GPA, socioeconomic status, on-campus employment, cognitive test scores, immediate, full-time college entry after high school, institutional control (public vs. private), ethnicity, gen-der, and intent to pursue a bachelor's degree.

[2]National Center for Education Statistics, 1997, Access to Postsecondary Education for the 1992 High School Graduates, *http://nces.ed.gov/pubs98/access/98105-7.asp*.

[3]*http://oldwww.bucks.edu/lifelong_learning/homeland.html*.

[4]Patricia Gunder, 2004, "Homeland Security and Civic Engagement: A Report of the Sec-ond Annual Summit." Available at *www.league.org/league/projects/homeland_security/files/ Homeland%20Security%20White%20Paper.pdf*.

AT THE UNDERGRADUATE LEVEL: ACCESS TO ALL CORE COURSES AND SOME ENRICHMENT EXPERIENCES

Not a single workshop participant, or any of the committee members, voiced support for an undergraduate degree program focused specifically on homeland security. As an area of study, it was deemed too immature and too broad. Several participants and committee members noted that given the enormous content variety in programs with such labels, it is unlikely that employers will even understand what any given "homeland security degree" represents. Moreover, such programs may give students a false impression that some professional consensus does exist about what actually constitutes knowledge of homeland security. Therefore, it is not recommended that a bachelor's degree in homeland security per se be offered. However, it is recommended that the core coursework identified above be available to undergraduate students and that they receive some recognition (e.g., a minor, concentration, or certificate) for completing it while working toward their major degree.

The preliminary Web survey of existing undergraduate programs (Appendix E) did not reveal any that appear to incorporate all five core elements in the context of an undergraduate minor, concentration, or certificate. Thus, attempting to offer the recommended core elements may be more difficult for undergraduate institutions than for community colleges, which generally had several—if not all—of the elements already in-house.

A particular difficulty in undergraduate instruction appears to be a lack of qualified instructors for the "core." Workshop participants who teach key courses (e.g., "history of terrorism," which falls under core component number three) state that they can accommodate only a small fraction of the students who wish to enroll. Typically, those outside the professor's home department are denied access. For an institution to provide instruction relevant to homeland security at the undergraduate level, the necessary coursework must be available to *all* prospective majors in *all* fields.

Beyond accessibility to the core coursework, there are additional educational experiences appropriate for undergraduates. The general consensus in the breakout sessions was that coursework emphasizing global and multicultural issues is appropriate. While terrorist acts themselves are not limited to foreign perpetrators, the substantial geographic isolation of the United States tends to diminish students' daily access to foreign points of view.

In addition to multicultural exposure, corporate, government, or nonprofit internships that give students exposure to the practice of homeland security were also strongly encouraged. Finally, given the complex, multidisciplinary nature of the threats that ultimately must be addressed

in homeland security, it is strongly recommended that students partici-
pate in a capstone course. Here, they would work for an extended period
of time (one course, spread over a semester or year) on a practical project
in a multidisciplinary team environment. One participant described, as
an example, the East-West Center, located in Hawaii, which allows students to interact with an international student body and learn firsthand
how to collaborate and cooperate as well as appreciate other cultures. This
kind of experience will prepare students for the many multidisciplinary
teams on which they will have to serve in the course of their careers and
ensure that the field of focus on homeland security does not become too
inwardly focused.

The committee notes that many of the extra experiences that it recommends for undergraduates—exposure to global issues, working on
multidisciplinary teams, and an emphasis on complex problem solving—
are foundational not only for homeland security but for twenty-first century work and life. The suggestions made here resonate highly with recommendations made by many educational bodies with regard to an
appropriate curriculum for the next century, for example, the Accreditation Board for Engineering and Technology (ABET) 2000 accreditation
guidelines and the National Academy of Engineering's report *The Engineer of 2020*.[5,6]

AT THE GRADUATE LEVEL (CERTIFICATES, MASTER'S, AND PROFESSIONAL MASTER'S): CORE PLUS SPECIALIZATION

Currently the Department of Homeland Security is providing competitive fellowships to 50 students per year in universities around the
country to pursue graduate degrees in multiple fields of science, engineering, and the humanities.[7] Workshops are available in the summer to
introduce students to careers in the homeland security area.[8] This seems
to be an appropriate way of supporting doctoral work toward DHS objectives. However, consistent with earlier National Academies work on federal programs, the DHS fellowship program, along with the Homeland
Security Centers of Excellence, should be assessed on a periodic basis to

---

[5]*http://www.abet.org/criteria.html*.

[6]National Academy of Engineering, 2004, *The Engineer of 2020*, Washington, D.C.: The National Academies Press.

[7]Department of Homeland Security Science and Technology Directorate's Homeland Security Fellowship Program for Students and Universities, *http://www.orau.gov/dhsed/default.htm*.

[8]Ibid.

establish goals and determine whether the programs are meeting those goals.[9] With respect to the fellowships program, such an evaluation might examine whether an alternative fellowship or traineeship program, such as the National Science Foundation's (NSF's) Integrative Graduate Education and Research Traineeship (IGERT) program, might more nearly meet the department's educational objectives at the doctoral level.

To the extent that an academic core for homeland security studies can be developed at the graduate level, it would be most appropriate that this material be formulated into a certificate program that could be available to graduate students enrolled in degree programs at the master's or Ph.D. levels. Such postbaccalaureate certificate programs are among the fastest-growing areas of higher education.[10] They are highly specific, typically geared toward the needs of employers, and usually accomplished within four or five courses. An example is the Certificate of Homeland Security offered by the University of Denver in concert with its master's degree in global studies (see Appendix E). The certificate program was designed for midcareer professionals, thoroughly treats core elements three and four, and touches on the other three core elements. The Homeland Security Certificate offered by the National Graduate School (see Appendix E) is another example, encompassing four of the five core elements, and touching only lightly on core element four. As the area of academic inquiry develops and workforce needs become more clearly defined, additional professional master's programs in aspects of homeland security studies will naturally develop to complement existing master's programs such as those listed in Appendix E.

AT THE EXECUTIVE LEVEL: EXECUTIVE TRAINING

At the executive level, the need is not just for multidisciplinary, multisectoral, multinational information access but also for managing, communicating, and coordinating multidisciplinary, multisectoral, multinational teams. The task is enormous and requires a shared strategic

---

[9]COSEPUP (Committee on Science, Engineering, and Public Policy), 1999, *Evaluating Federal Research Programs: Research and the Government Performance and Results Act,* Washington, D.C.: National Academy Press.

[10]Wayne Patterson, 2001, "Ensuring the Quality of Certificate Programs," *Continuing Higher Education Review,* Fall:112-127.

vision, a common culture, a mutually understood language, and an extensive network of professional contacts across many boundaries. The most logical way to provide these capabilities is through shared executive training.

Identified as one of the key areas for training by participants at a breakout session, executive training can create a common culture across upper management for handling homeland security issues, regardless of the location or institution represented by that management. For the individual, executive training can provide strategic skills, transfer lessons learned from other executives, upgrade resource management capabilities, and, of course, generate useful personal contacts. As a starting point, executive training courses could further the evolution of the 22 original agencies comprising the Department of Homeland Security into a cohesive organization. It can then bring together senior DHS management with their counterparts in other government agencies and the private sector to generate a shared vision, communication strategy, and team functionality. Finally, training with executives in other nations may well provide the critical personal linkages needed to confront individual threats as they arise. Jim Keagle and Steve Duncan of the National Defense University (NDU) pointed out that the six-week "CAPSTONE" course offered by NDU was structured to accomplish these goals for senior military personnel across the armed forces, and a similar structure could be envisioned for satisfying the executive education needs across the federal/state/local agencies and institutions currently responsible for homeland security.

Summary

If homeland security is understood to be the protection of the U.S. peoples against extreme, unanticipated threats, it becomes apparent that the design of an educational counterpart has an extremely broad, multidisciplinary, and still-evolving mandate. Accordingly, the committee—based in large part on discussions at a one-day workshop but also on further reading and research—proposes that homeland security educational initiatives contain a small core of content that builds an intellectual framework for threat assessment and threat management. This framework can and should be applied to the multiple rich opportunities that exist within in the context of individual disciplines (undergraduate) and multidisciplinary research and training experiences (graduate). In addition, there are opportunities to encourage executive training for those entrusted with managing the homeland security strategies of institutions, regions, and nations.

The present state of experimentation among graduate and undergraduate programs is seen as a strength rather than a weakness. Neither workshop attendees nor committee members voiced support for an all-definitive, all-encompassing "Homeland Security University," or for the development of independent academic tracks specializing exclusively in homeland security. Further interaction and feedback between fledgling programs and the communities they serve should gradually refine academic definitions and approaches over time to concepts that are enduring and meaningful. Meanwhile, as concepts, practices, and institutions in homeland security evolve, the higher education community should continue to serve its traditional function of promoting debate and productive social criticism about such directions.

Appendix A

Committee Member Biographies

Irwin Feller (*Committee Chair*) is currently a senior visiting scientist at the American Association for the Advancement of Science, having recently completed 24 years as the director of Penn State's Institute for Policy Research and Evaluation. He also serves as a professor emeritus of Penn State's Department of Economics, where he was on the faculty for nearly three decades. Dr. Feller received his Ph.D. in economics from the University of Minnesota and his B.A. in economics from the City University of New York.

Dr. Feller has a long history of publishing scholarly articles on organizational structure and function and its effect on the creation of knowledge and societal benefits, using both universities and government programs as objects of study. This expertise has been applied to problems of the nucleation and growth of new scientific fields, to the anatomy and function of interdisciplinary research programs, to the effectiveness of various technology transfer mechanisms, to the metrics used to evaluate research in government programs, and to a host of other mechanisms and institutions of importance to the scientific enterprise. Dr. Feller has served on six National Academies committees. From 2002 to 2004, Irwin Feller served as the chair of the National Science Foundation's Advisory Committee to the Assistant Director of Social, Behavioral, and Economic Sciences, a committee of which he has been a member since 1999.

Johnnie Carson joined the National Defense University as senior vice president in August 2003 upon his return from the Republic of Kenya, where he served as U.S. ambassador from August 1999 to July 2003. During his tour in Kenya, Ambassador Carson was responsible for rebuilding and restoring full diplomatic services at the U.S. embassy in Nairobi following its destruction by terrorists in 1998. Prior to this assignment to Kenya, he served as principal deputy assistant secretary for the Bureau of African Affairs at the Department of State. Ambassador Carson is a career member of the Senior Foreign Service, Class of Career Minister. Ambassador Carson has also served as the U.S. ambassador to Zimbabwe (1995-1997) and to Uganda (1991-1994).

Ambassador Carson served as staff officer in the staff secretariat in the Office of the Secretary of State from 1978 to 1979. He held the assignment of deputy political counselor at the American Embassy in Lisbon, Portugal, from 1982 to 1986. Before joining the Foreign Service, Mr. Carson was a Peace Corps volunteer in Tanzania from 1965 to 1968.

Ambassador Carson received his undergraduate education from Drake University where he earned a bachelor of arts in history and political science and his graduate education from the School of Oriental and Africa Studies at the University of London where he was awarded a master of arts in international relations. Ambassador Carson is the recipient of several Superior Honor Awards from the Department of State and a Meritorious Service Award from Secretary of State Madeleine Albright. The Centers for Disease Control and Prevention presented Ambassador Carson its highest award, Champion of Prevention Award, for his leadership in directing the U.S. government's HIV/AIDS prevention efforts in Kenya.

Max M. Houck currently uses his expertise as a trace evidence expert and forensic anthropologist in his capacity as director for the Forensic Science Initiative at West Virginia University (WVU). Using the technology incubator at WVU, Max Houck has also formed the nonprofit Institute for Cold Case Evaluation, providing police with free or discounted assistance from at least two dozen of the country's top behind-the-scenes forensic scientists. Just before he joined WVU, Mr. Houck was assigned to Dover Air Force Base, Delaware, to assist with identification of the victims of the 9/11 Pentagon attack. Mr. Houck worked on more than 800 other cases in his assignment to the Federal Bureau of Investigations (FBI) laboratory from 1992 to 2001. He has been the recipient of both a Quality Award from the FBI laboratory and the American Society of Testing and Materials Forensic Science Award in 2000.

Prior to his career at the FBI, Mr. Houck was the forensic anthropologist and a trace evidence examiner at the Medical Examiner's Office in Fort Worth, Texas. While at that office, he coordinated the anthropological recovery and scientific examinations of the Branch Davidian compound near Waco, Texas. Mr. Houck is a graduate of Michigan State University and a fellow of the American Academy of Forensic Sciences, among other professional organizations. He has coauthored and edited two books of forensic case reviews, *Mute Witnesses* (2001) and *Trace Evidence Analysis* (2003), published by Academic Press. Currently, he is working on an upper-level introductory forensic science textbook.

Heather Kiriakou graduated with an M.A. in security studies from Georgetown University in 2003. From 1997 to the present, Ms. Kiriakou has worked as a Middle East analyst for the Central Intelligence Agency (CIA) where she has earned several awards for her exceptional performance. Prior to her work at the CIA, Ms. Kiriakou received a B.S. degree in foreign service and worked for two years as a program manager at the Office of the Secretary of Defense, managing the Mentor-Protégé program. Currently Ms. Kiriakou is in the midst of a one-year term as an intelligence fellow with the Council on Foreign Relations. She has expertise in Middle Eastern politics, strategy, and leadership dynamics; intelligence; and national security.

Arie W. Kruglanski is a social psychologist specializing in how people form judgments, beliefs, impressions, and attitudes and what consequences this has for their interpersonal relations, their interaction in groups, and their feelings about various "out groups." A major academic contribution has been Dr. Kruglanski's formulation of a theory of lay epistemics that specifies how thought and motivation interface in the formation of subjective knowledge. His work on this and related topics has been disseminated in more than 150 articles, chapters, and books and has been supported continuously by grants from the National Science Foundation and the National Institute of Mental Health. Dr. Kruglanski has a broad perspective on what is known and not known about the social science aspects of terrorism, having previously served on the National Research Council (NRC) committee that authored the reports, *Terrorism: Perspectives from the Behavioral and Social Sciences* and *Discouraging Terrorism: Implications of 9/11.*

Dr. Kruglanski is the recipient of the National Institute of Mental Health Research Scientist Award, the Humboldt Forschungspreis (life achievement award), and the Donald Campbell Award for Outstanding Contributions to Social Psychology. He was a fellow at the Center for Advanced Study in the Behavioral Sciences and is a fellow of both the American Psychological Association and the American Psychological Society. He has served as associate editor of *American Psychologist* and as chief editor of the *Personality and Social Psychology Bulletin* and the *Journal of Personality and Social Psychology: Attitudes and Social Cognition* section.

Monica Schoch-Spana is a medical anthropologist. Prior to joining the University of Pittsburgh Medical Center (UPMC), she worked for five years at the Johns Hopkins Center for Civilian Biodefense Strategies. Dr. Schoch-Spana received her B.A. from Bryn Mawr College in 1986 and her Ph.D. in cultural anthropology from the Johns Hopkins University in 1998. In recent years, Dr. Schoch-Spana has performed extensive scholarly work on community responses to and public communication needs during terrorist attacks and health crises. Her scientific investigations of relevant case studies include the 1918 pandemic influenza, the 1999 West Nile Virus, the 2001 World Trade Center attacks, and the anthrax letters crisis. Select publications include "Bioterrorism and the Public: How to Vaccinate a City Against Panic," "Clinical Infectious Diseases, 2002," and "Educating, Informing and Mobilizing the Public," in *Terrorism and Public Health,* B. Levy and V. Sidel, eds., Oxford University Press, 2002, 2003. Recently she organized the 2003 national leadership summit "The Public as an Asset, Not a Problem."

Dr. Schoch-Spana also chairs the Working Group on Governance Dilemmas in Bioterrorism Response, a group charged with enhancing the ability of mayors, governors, and health authorities to reduce the disruptive quality of biological attacks and government responses to them. She is additionally a principal investigator for a national study of public communication experiences during the anthrax attacks and has served as a technical adviser to the Ad Council's national campaign on emergency preparedness.

Debra Stewart is president of the Council of Graduate Schools, the leading national organization dedicated to the improvement and advancement of graduate education. Dr. Stewart has a Ph.D. in political science from the University of North Carolina, Chapel Hill. Until July 2000, when she joined the Council of Graduate Schools, she was vice chancellor and dean of the Graduate School at North Carolina State University. She also served as interim chancellor at the University of North Carolina at Greensboro. Dr. Stewart has been an active leader in higher education nationally as chair of the Board of Directors of the Council of Graduate Schools, the Graduate Record Examination Board, the Council on Research Policy and Graduate Education, and the Board of Directors of Oak Ridge Associated Universities. She also served as vice chair of the Board of Trustees of the Educational Testing Service and as a trustee of the Triangle University Center for Advanced Studies. Dr. Stewart was a member of the NRC Committee on the Assessment of the Research Doctorate and currently serves on the NRC's Board on Higher Education and Workforce, the Advisory Board for the Carnegie Initiative on the Doctorate, the Advisory Council for the Responsive Ph.D. Project, and the American Council on Education

Board. She also chairs the Steering Committee of the Higher Education Secretariat in Washington.

Dr. Stewart is author, coauthor, and editor of books and numerous scholarly articles on administrative theory and public policy. She lectures internationally on graduate education issues and challenges. Her research focuses on ethics in managerial decision making. Her recent work, supported by the National Science Foundation, explored attitudes and moral reasoning styles among public officials in Poland and Russia.

Appendix B

Workshop Agenda

Educational Paradigms for Homeland Security
April 26, 2004
Keck Building, Rm. 100
500 Fifth St., N.W.
Washington, DC 20001

8:00-8:10   Greetings
             Irwin Feller, Senior Visiting Scientist, American Association
             for the Advancement of Science and Workshop Committee
             Chair

8:10-8:20   Introduction to the Workshop
             Melvin Bernstein, Director, Office of University Programs,
             Department of Homeland Security

8:20-8:45   National Needs, University Needs, and Homeland
             Security
             Joseph B. Hellige, Vice Provost for Academic Programs,
             University of Southern California

8:45-9:15   FEMA Higher Education Project
             B. Wayne Blanchard, Higher Education Project Manager,
             Emergency Management Institute, Federal Emergency
             Management Agency

9:15-9:30   Break

9:30-11:30   Homeland Security: A Multidisciplinary Panel Discussion
             Moderator: *Debra Stewart*, President, Council of Graduate
             Schools and Workshop Committee Member
             • *Stephen E. Flynn*, Jeane J. Kirkpatrick Senior Fellow,
               Council on Foreign Relations
             • *Susan L. Cutter*, Director, Hazards Research Laboratory,
               Department of Geography, University of South Carolina
             • *William L, Waugh, Jr.* Professor of Public Administration,
               Urban Studies, and Political Science, Georgia State
               University
             • *Martha Crenshaw*, Colin and Nancy Campbell Professor
               of Global Issues and Democratic Thought, Wesleyan
               University

11:30-1:00 Lunch and Breakout Session I

             Breakout groups to be chaired by the following workshop
             committee members:
             Group A (Rm. 205)
             • *Johnnie Carson*, Senior Vice President, National Defense
               University
             Group B (Rm. 201)
             • *Max M. Houck*, Director, Forensic Identification
               Program, West Virginia University
             Group C (Rm. 206)
             • *Heather Kiriakou*, Intelligence Fellow, Council on Foreign
               Relations
             Group D (Rm. 100)
             • *Arie W. Kruglanski*, Distinguished Professor of
               Psychology, University of Maryland
             Group E (Rm. 213)
             • *Monica Schoch-Spana*, Senior Fellow, University of
               Pittsburgh Medical Center (UPMC) Center for
               Biosecurity

All breakout groups to discuss the following question:

             Are there genuine, unmet educational needs in homeland
             security—either in terms of workforce skills or in terms of
             public outreach? If so, what are they?

1:00-1:30   Breakout Session I Reports
              Moderator: *Irwin Feller*, Senior Visiting Scientist, American
                 Association for the Advancement of Science and
                 Workshop Committee Chair

1:30-2:00   Afternoon Plenary: National Defense University (NDU)
              Education and the Changing National Security
              Environment
              Introductions: *Johnnie Carson*, Senior Vice President, NDU
              Plenary Presentation: *Steve M. Duncan*, Distinguished
              Fellow, and
              Jim M. Keagle, Vice President for Academic Affairs, NDU

2:00-3:30   Breakout Sessions II

              *Breakout session chairs comprise the same workshop committee
              members as previously. Each breakout session group to be given
              a different list of question or issues to respond to, as follows:*

              Group A (*Johnnie Carson*, Chair, Rm. 205):
              • What do current homeland security educational
                programs encompass, and why are they important?
              • What areas should such programs encompass that are
                not necessarily obvious?
              • What are the differences between existing social science,
                political science, or natural science degree programs
                and potential or current homeland security curricula?

              Group B (*Max M. Houck*, Chair, Rm. 201):
              • What kinds of careers would a university-based
                homeland security education prepare one for?

              Group C (*Heather Kiriakou*, Chair, Rm. 206):
              • What parallelisms can one draw between the post-9/11
                emergence of academic offerings in homeland security
                and the emergence of area studies, international
                relations, and science policy in the Cold War era?

Group D (*Arie Kruglanski*, Chair, Rm. 100)
- With respect to developing workforce skills, to what extent should homeland security curricula be uniform versus specialized? What core skills should all workers in this area (however it is defined) have? If there needs to be additional specialization around the core, what might be areas of specialization and how would they be integrated into the curriculum?
- What are the most important unanswered questions with respect to homeland security educational issues?

Group E (*Monica Shoch-Spana*, Chair, Rm. 213)
- What curricular content is or should be unique to homeland security, and what is or would be a repackaging of existing material?
- Is homeland security inherently an emerging discipline of its own, or is it better characterized as an interdisciplinary thrust?

3:30-4:25   Breakout Session II Reports
             Moderator: *Debra Stewart*, President, Council of Graduate Schools and Workshop Committee Member

4:25-4:30   Summary Comments
             Melvin Bernstein, Director, Office of University Programs, Department of Homeland Security

4:30-4:35   Closing Comments
             Irwin Feller, Senior Visiting Scientist, American Association for the Advancement of Science and Workshop Committee Chair

Appendix
C

Workshop Speaker Biographies

Melvin Bernstein joined the Office of Research and Development in the Science and Technology Directorate of the Department of Homeland Security (DHS) on June 1, 2003, as director of university programs. Dr. Bernstein comes to DHS from Tufts University, where he is currently a research professor in the Department of Mechanical Engineering. Previously, he served as professor and head of the Department of Metallurgy and Materials Science at Carnegie-Mellon University; provost and then chancellor at the Illinois Institute of Technology; academic vice president and dean of the faculties at Tufts University; and most recently, provost and senior vice president for academic affairs at Brandeis University. Other relevant experiences includes liaison scientist at the London Office of the Office of Naval Research; member of the National Materials Advisory Board of the National Research Council; and panel chair of the National Research Council study, *Materials Science and Engineering for the 1990s*.

B. Wayne Blanchard is the manager of the Federal Emergency Management Agency's Emergency Management Higher Education Project. The primary purpose of this project is to encourage and support the development of undergraduate and graduate degrees and programs in the subjects of hazards, disasters, and emergency management in colleges and universities across the country. Dr. Blanchard has been with the Emergency Management Institute since May 1994. Prior to his current assignment, Dr. Blanchard worked in the National Preparedness Directorate and the State and Local Programs Support Directorate. A major contribution in these earlier years was the creation of the Family Disaster Preparedness Program, now known as the Community and Family Preparedness Program. Among Dr. Blanchard's disaster assignments have been Hurricane Andrew, the Midwest floods of 1993, and the Northridge earthquake of January 1994. As part of a citizen disaster preparedness campaign, he also produced approximately 50 videotaped public service announcements using the donated time of more than 24 Hollywood celebrities.

Dr. Blanchard has a B.A. in political science and history (with honors) from the University of North Carolina at Charlotte, a master's in international affairs from the University of Virginia, and a Ph.D. in government and foreign affairs from the University of Virginia.

Martha Crenshaw is the Colin and Nancy Campbell Professor of Global Issues and Democratic Thought and professor of government at Wesleyan University, in Middletown, Connecticut, where she has taught since 1974. She has written extensively on the issue of political terrorism; her first article, "The Concept of Revolutionary Terrorism," was published in the *Journal of Conflict Resolution* in 1972.

Her recent work includes the chapter "Coercive Diplomacy and the Response to Terrorism," in *The United States and Coercive Diplomacy*, published by the United States Institute of Peace (2003), and "Terrorism, Strategies, and Grand Strategies," in *The Campaign Against International Terrorism* published by Georgetown University Press (2004). She serves on the Executive Board of Women in International Security and on the Council of the American Political Science Association. She is a former president of the International Society of Political Psychology.

Susan L. Cutter is a Carolina Distinguished Professor of Geography at the University of South Carolina. She is also the director of the Hazards Research Lab, a research and training center that integrates geographical information science with hazard analysis and management. She received her B.A. from California State University and her M.A. and Ph.D. from the University of Chicago. Dr. Cutter has been working in the risk and hazards field for more than 25 years and is a nationally recognized scholar in this field. Her primary research interests are in the area of vulnerability science—What makes people and the places in which they live vulnerable to extreme events and how is this measured and monitored? She has authored or edited 11 books and more than 75 peer-reviewed articles and book chapters. Dr. Cutter is also the co-founding editor of an interdisciplinary journal, *Environmental Hazards.*

In 1999, Dr. Cutter was elected as a fellow of the American Association for the Advancement of Science, a testimonial to her research accomplishments in the field. Her stature within the discipline of geography was recognized by her election as president of the Association of American Geographers in 1999-2000. She serves on many national advisory boards and committees, including those of the National Research Council.

Stephen M. Duncan is a distinguished fellow at the National Defense University (NDU), Fort McNair, Washington, D.C. His work is focused on homeland security, military strategy and force structure, and civil-military relations. He is the author of three books on these topics. Prior to his arrival at NDU, Mr. Duncan served as the president and chief executive officer of a systems engineering and information technology company. Previously, Mr. Duncan served as assistant secretary of defense for reserve affairs from 1997 to 1993. In this capacity he was responsible for all matters involving the reserve components, including the mobilization of the 222,000 reservists called to duty during the Persian Gulf War of 1990-1991. From April 1989 to January 1993, Mr. Duncan also served separately as the Department of Defense coordinator for drug enforcement policy and support. In that capacity, he was responsible for all international and domestic policies and actions involving the use of the Armed Forces to carry out counterdrug missions.

During his time at the Pentagon, Mr. Duncan testified in more than 50 congressional hearings on a wide range of matters related to policies involving the reserve components and the administration's counterdrug programs. Mr. Duncan has also served in the legal profession, both in private practice and as an assistant U.S. attorney for the federal district of Colorado. Mr. Duncan is a highly decorated veteran of the Vietnam War, a fellow of the International Society of Barristers, a member of the faculty of the National Trial Advocacy College at the University of Virginia School of Law, and a former assistant professor of naval science at Dartmouth College. Mr. Duncan holds a bachelor of science degree from the U.S. Naval Academy, a master of arts degree in American government from Dartmouth College, and a doctor of jurisprudence degree from the University of Colorado.

Stephen E. Flynn is the Jeane J. Kirkpatrick Senior Fellow for National Security Studies at the Council on Foreign Relations, a leading expert on port and container security, and a noted authority on homeland security. Dr. Flynn serves as the principal adviser to the bipartisan congressional Port Security Caucus. In his position at the Council on Foreign Relations, Dr. Flynn directs a project on terror and the unprotected homeland. He served as director of the Office of Global Issues, National Security Council, and was a consultant to both the U.S. Commission on National Security/21st Century (the Hart-Rudman commission) and the White House Office of Emergency Operations.

Dr. Flynn was a member of the National Academy of Sciences Panel on Science and Technology for Countering Terrorism in Transportation and Distribution Systems in 2002. Earlier, he served as guest scholar and project co-director of the Foreign Policy Studies Program at the Brookings Institution and as adjunct fellow and project director of the Political-Military Program and the Americas Program at the Center for Strategic and International Studies. Dr. Flynn also held a position as associate professor of international relations at the U.S. Coast Guard Academy, responsible for curriculum development and instruction in international relations, national security policy, drug policy, and global policy studies. A 1982 graduate of the U.S. Coast Guard Academy, Dr. Flynn retired with the rank of commander after 20 years of active duty service.

Joseph B. Hellige is vice provost for academic programs, dean of the Graduate School, and professor in the Department of Psychology at the University of Southern California (USC). As vice provost, Dr. Hellige serves as the senior executive officer responsible to the provost for all university academic programs. As a faculty member in the Department of Psychology, Dr. Hellige has published two books and approximately 100 articles in scholarly journals on a variety of topics in cognitive psychology and neuropsychology. From 1992 to 1997 he also served as the department chair, before assuming his first vice provost position as vice provost of undergraduate studies. Dr. Hellige's primary research interests include information processing differences between the left and right cerebral hemispheres in humans.

Dr. Hellige has been a fellow or member of numerous professional organizations, including the American Psychological Association, the Psychonomic Society, the American Psychological Society, the International Neuropsychological Society, the Cognitive Neuroscience Society, the American Academy for the Advancement of Science, and the American Association for Higher Education. Dr. Hellige has also been honored as Graduate Mentor of the Year by the Graduate Association of Students in Psychology at USC and has received the Albert S. Raubenheimer Award for Excellence in Teaching, Research, and Service from the College of Letters, Arts, and Sciences at USC. Dr. Hellige received his B.A. degree from Saint Mary's College of Minnesota and his M.A. and Ph.D. degrees in psychology from the University of Wisconsin, Madison.

James M. Keagle is an expert in professional military education, currently serving as vice president for academic affairs at the National Defense University (NDU). His responsibilities include oversight of NDU's four graduate-level colleges, two research institutes, three regional centers, and the NDU library, which was ranked first in the U.S. government system in 2002. His responsibilities include curriculum development, hiring and nonrenewal decisions, registrar functions, and all academic items within NDU's $100 million budget. Prior to taking the vice presidential post, Dr. Keagle served as NDU's dean for academic affairs.

Dr. Keagle's familiarity with educational issues is rooted in nine years of full-time teaching for the professional military education system, including three years at the National War College as a professor of national security policy and director of Latin American studies and six years as a faculty member in the Department of Political Science at the U.S. Air Force Academy. For an overlapping 25 years, Dr. Keagle has simultaneously served as an adjunct professor for several external institutions. Early in his career, he worked in the Office of the Secretary of Defense, specializing in issues related to Cuba and Bosnia. His formal education includes a Ph.D. in politics from Princeton and two M.A.s: one in politics from Princeton and a second in political science from the University of Pittsburgh. Dr. Keagle has published two books on policy and the political process, as well as numerous articles and book reviews.

William L. Waugh, Jr., is professor of public administration, urban studies, and political science in the Andrew Young School of Policy Studies at Georgia State University in Atlanta. He is the author of *Living with Hazards, Dealing with Disasters* (2000), *Terrorism and Emergency Management* (1990), and *International Terrorism* (1982) and is coeditor of *Disaster Management in the US and Canada* (1996), *Cities and Disaster* (1990), and *Handbook of Emergency Management* (1990).

Dr. Waugh has been a consultant to public, private, and nonprofit organizations and the media on dealing with terrorist threats and other disasters and increasing governmental and nongovernmental capacities for managing hazards and disasters. He has taught graduate and undergraduate courses on terrorism and emergency management for more than 25 years. He has developed courses for the Federal Emergency Management Agency, provided emergency management training programs for local agencies, and conducted studies on topics ranging from network roles in encouraging safe construction to dealing with workplace violence and terrorism. He has served three times as chair of the American Society for Public Administration's Section on Emergency and Crisis Management and currently serves on the Certified Emergency Manager Commission (International Association of Emergency Managers) and the Emergency Management Accreditation Program Commission (Council of State Governments).

Appendix
D

Workshop Participants

Jameel Ahmad
Cooper Union

Chris Bellavita
Naval Postgraduate School

Judith Bernstein
Corinthian Colleges, Inc.

Mel Bernstein
Department of Homeland Security

Constance Blackwood
Universities Space Research
   Association

Wayne Blanchard
Federal Emergency Management
   Agency

David Brych
The Aerospace Corporation

Daniel Byram
Corinthian Colleges, Inc.

Johnnie Carson
National Defense University

Alok Chaturvedi
Purdue University

Frank Cilluffo
George Washington University

Martha Crenshaw
Wesleyan University

W. David Cummings
Universities Space Research
   Association

Susan Cutter
University of South Carolina

Shana Dale
Office of Science and Technlogy
   Policy

Adrian Del Caro
University of Colorado

Steve Duncan
National Defense University

Laura Ewing
Department of Homeland Security

Richard Ewing
Texas A&M University

Irwin Feller
Pennsylvania State University

Ed Furtek
University of California, San
    Diego

Stephen Flynn
Council on Foreign Relations

Stephen F. Gambescia
Drexel University

Howard Garrison
Federation of American Societies
    for Experimental Biology

Asha George
ANSER Institute for Homeland
    Security

John Gerner
Federal Highway Adminstration

Howard Greenstein
New York University

Joyce Gross
National Oceanic and
    Atmospheric Administration

John Harrald
George Washington University

Joe Hellige
University of Southern California

Max Houck
West Virginia University

Carol Hudgings
National Institutes of Health

Robert Jaffin
American Public University
    System

Wyn Jennings
Department of Homeland Security

Thomas Johnson
New Haven University

Daniel Kaniewski
George Washington University

Jim Keagle
National Defense University

Philip Kenul
National Oceanic and
    Atmospheric Administration

Paul Kincade
Federation of American Societies
    for Experimental Biology

Heather Kiriakou
Council on Foreign Relations

Arie Kruglanski
University of Maryland, College
    Park

Sheryl Maddox
U.S. Department of Agriculture

Audrey Martini
Michigan State University
School of Criminal Justice

Aileen Marty
Department of Homeland Security

Daniel McBride
Kaplan College

Maureen McCarthy
Department of Homeland Security

Kera McGinn
Department of Homeland Security

Robert McGrath
Pennsylvania State University

John Miller
U.S. Department of Energy

J. Strother Moore
University of Texas

James Moore
University of Southern California

Greg Moser
Institute on Globalization and
    Security
Denver University

Terry Nipp
National Institute for Agricultural
    Security

Nancy Oesch
Florida Metropolitan University

Laura Olson
George Washington University

Laura Petonito
Department of Homeland Security

John Pine
Louisiana State University

Uday Ram
Council on Foreign Relations

Claire Rubin
George Washington University

Susan Sayles
Corinthian Colleges, Inc.

Michael Schatz
Georgia Institute of Technology

Monica Schoch-Spana
University of Pittsburgh Medical
    Center
Center for Biosecurity

Samuel Seymour
Johns Hopkins University
Applied Physics Laboratory

Eric Sheppard
Hampton University

Debra Stewart
Council of Graduate Schools

Todd Stewart
National Academic Consortium
    for Homeland Security
Ohio State University

Kelly Sullivan
Pacific Northwest National
    Laboratory

Keith Thompson
Office of the Deputy Under
    Secretary of Defense

Keith Voorhees
American Chemical Society

Joseph Vorbach
U.S. Coast Guard Academy

Karen Walker
Department of Homeland Security

William Waugh
Georgia State University

Meegan White
Association of Public Television
    Stations

Rae Zimmerman
New York University

Appendix
E
Sample Organizations Offering Homeland Security Education Programs

University/Organization	Type of Program	Contact Information	Background Descriptions of Program
American Institute of Homeland Defense	Education and training programs	Melvin Reid American Institute of Homeland Defense P.O. Box 357 Grandview, TX 76050 Tel.: (817) 975-2411 Tel.: (800) 518-2728 Email: *reidm@americanihd.com*	The American Institute of Homeland Defense (AIHD) has instructed in excess of 18,000 law enforcement, military, medical, and corporate personnel. AIHD is the leader in certified / credit-bearing homeland security education and training programs. Certified workforce education college credit courses : • Solutions for Law Enforcement • Solutions for Medical Personnel • Solutions for Fire Department Personnel • Solutions for Organizations and Security Forces
American Military University	Graduate and undergraduate homeland security certificate programs	Robert Jaffin Department Chair, Public Sector and Critical Infrastructure Studies American Public University System 111 West Congress St. Charles Town , WV 25414 Tel.: (304) 724-3723 Fax: 304 724-3786 Email: *bjaffin@apus.edu* *http://www.apus.edu*	Core courses for the graduate certificate include: • Consequence Management: Terrorism Preparation and Response • Quarantine • Intelligence and Homeland Security • Forecasting Terrorism • Homeland Defense • Comparative Homeland Security Undergraduate core courses similar.

ANSER Institute for Homeland Security

Executive education and internships

Dr. Asha M. George
Manager Director
ANSER Institute for Homeland Security
2900 South Quincy St.
Suite 800
Arlington, VA 22206
Tel.: (703) 416-3597
Fax: (703) 416-3126
Email: *institute.director@anser.org*

Executive Education Program

Teaching homeland security courses in cooperation with the Johns Hopkins University, George Washington University, U.S. National War College, and U.S. National Graduate School. The curriculum will address current and potential real-world problems that pose challenges to executives seeking to manage threats to the homeland. Topic areas will include:

- Analytical problem-solving skills obtained through modeling and exercises (tabletop)
- Asymmetric and symmetric warfare/conflicts
- Civilian/military relationship building
- Critical infrastructure protection
- Complexities/responsibilities of coordinated efforts between federal, state, local, and private sectors
- Computing and intelligence issues
- Deterrence and threat reduction
- Incident management systems (local, state, and federal)
- Law enforcement and judicial issues
- Media management
- Public health concerns
- Research design and data analysis skills
- Seminar, tabletop, drill, and exercise design
- Threat and vulnerability assessments

continued

University/Organization	Type of Program	Contact Information	Background Descriptions of Program
			University Alliances Program: The University Alliances program will actively encourage the recruitment of interns to the mutual benefit of the participating universities and the institute. The internship program will provide interns with real-world experiences dealing with homeland security issues critical for successful translation from theory-based to practice-based educational objectives.
Cooper Union	Graduate certificate in urban security	Prof. Jameel Ahmad Professor and Chair Department of Civil Engineering Cooper Union for the Advancement of Science and Art Cooper Square New York, NY 10003-7120 Tel.: (212) 353-4294 Email: *ahmad@cooper.edu*	Required courses: • Urban Security • Structural Dynamics • Advanced Structural Design
Corinthian Colleges, Inc., including: • Blair College Inc. • Florida Metropolitan University-Brandon • Florida Metropolitan University-Pinellas • Florida Metropolitan University-Pompano • Florida Metropolitan	Homeland security specialist programs, including A.S. and B.S. degrees	Daniel Byram Corinthian Colleges, Inc. Director of Security, Justice and Legal Programs 6 Hutton Centre Dr., Suite 400 Santa Ana, CA 92707-5764 Tel.: (714) 427-3000 Ext 201 Email: *dbyram@cci.edu*	Programs of study (7 months): • Civil and Criminal Justice • Emergency Planning and Security Measures • Homeland Security: Principles, Planning, and Procedures • Tactical Communications • Domestic and International Terrorism • Emergency Medical Services and Fire Operations

- Business and Ethics for Security Specialists

University-South Orlando
- Florida Metropolitan University-Tampa
- National Institute of Technology-Cross Lanes
- Parks Business College
- Parks College-Thornton

Drexel University Goodwin College of Professional Studies

Professional development coursework in homeland security and emergency management; development of A.S. and B.S. degrees in progress.

Stephen F. Gambescia, Assistant Dean/Associate Professor Drexel University Goodwin College of Professional Studies 3001 Market St., Suite 100 Philadelphia, PA 19104 Tel.: (215) 895-0909 Email: *stephen.f.gambescia@drexel.edu* *http://www.drexel.edu/academics/goodwin/homeland Security.asp*

51 six-hour Skill Enhancement Training seminars: A competency-based training and education series for professionals employed in public and private entities responsible for security and public safety. Courses focus on terrorism, disaster emergency management, facilities security, hazardous materials, incident command and control, IT security and laws, regulations, and public administration.

- Disaster Emergency Management Courses
- Facilities Security Courses
- Hazardous Materials Courses
- Incident Command and Control Courses
- IT Security Specialist
- Laws, Regulations, and Public Administration Courses
- Terrorism Courses

continued

University/Organization	Type of Program	Contact Information	Background Descriptions of Program
			The courses will build on established certification training programs such as those offered by local police and fire academies, as well as programs for emergency medical technicians, hazardous material handlers, municipal emergency management professionals, public security organizations, and private safety and security providers.
			The courses also can lead to a new emergency management and panning program at the associate's and bachelor's degree levels.
George Washington University	Master's, certificate, and Ph.D. degrees in 28 fields closely related to homeland security; also a separate policy forum (see *http://www. homelandsecurity.gwu. edu/dhs/programs/ edu.html* for complete list)	Frank J. Cilluffo Associate Vice President for Homeland Security The George Washington University 2300 I St. NW, Suite 721 Washington, DC 20037 Tel.: (202) 994-0295 Email: *cilluffo@gwu.edu* Daniel Kaniewski Deputy Director Homeland Security Policy Institute and Executive Director Center for Emergency Preparedness The George Washington University	Examples of degrees: • Master of science in public health, microbiology, and emerging infectious diseases • Ph.D. in public policy and administration, national security policy • Graduate certificate, telecommunication and national security • Master of science in civil and mechanical engineering, transportation Safety engineering • Doctor of science in engineering management, focus in crisis, emergency, and risk management

Medical Center
2300 Eye St. NW, Suite 721
Washington, DC 20037
Tel.: (202) 994-2437
Email: *dankan@gwu.edu*
http://homelandsecurity.gwu.edu/

The Homeland Security Policy Institute (HSPI)

- Draws on the expertise of the George Washington University and its partners from the academic, nonprofit, policy, and private sectors for a common goal of better preparing the nation for the threat of terrorism.
- HSPI frames the debate, discusses policy implications and alternatives, and recommends solutions to issues facing America's homeland security policymakers.
- Builds a bridge between theory and practice in the homeland security arena.

Grantham University

Gary Sutter
Academic Dean
34641 Grantham Rd.
Slidell, LA 70460
Tel.: (800) 955-2527 ext 252
Email: *sutterg@grantham.edu*

B.S. in criminal justice, with specialization in homeland security

The program focuses on an interdisciplinary set of topics associated with homeland security, including:

- psychology of terrorism
- forecasting terrorism
- terrorism and counterterrorism
- border and coastal security
- terrorism and U.S. national security
- emergency planning

continued

University/Organization	Type of Program	Contact Information	Background Descriptions of Program
Houston Community College (HCC)	Continuing education courses, certificates, and an associate degree in applied sciences specializing in homeland security	Louis Duran Security Chief Houston Community College System 3100 Main St. Houston, TX, 77002 Mail code 1611 Tel.: (713) 718-7560 Email: louis.duran@hccs.edu	HCC, as part of a consortium with several other community colleges in Texas, offers training by former military, FBI, and CIA personnel brought in by the American Institute of Homeland Defense. The college offers 60 eight-hour continuing education courses in such topics as intelligence operations, decontamination, and terrorist profiling. Most of the courses are open to the general public but are targeted toward police, firefighters, and first responders. Students complete nine of 12 courses to earn certification in such areas as understanding and combating terrorism; emergency management; and investigating, preventing, and surviving terrorism for law enforcement.
Indiana University of Pennsylvania, John P. Murtha Institute for Homeland Security	Master's degree program in the science of emergency response; bachelor's-level track in cyber security; continuing education in weapons of mass destruction	Thomas Dalton Indiana University of Pennsylvania Institute for Homeland Security University Towers 850 Maple St. Indiana, PA 15705 Tel.: (724) 357-3110 Email: tdalton@iup.edu	Master of science in science of disaster response The MS in science of disaster response is a 32-credit nonthesis degree that has been developed specifically for the WMD response community. The 18 credit core consists of 12 credits of intensive lecture and laboratory sessions in biology, chemistry, and nuclear physics/radiology and a six (6) credit advanced field experience in disaster response. Students earn the remaining 14

credits in required courses. Currently, all the required courses are lecture-only courses, except for SDR 610 Advanced Techniques in Biotechnology for Disaster Response, which provides both lecture and laboratory experiences.

Continuing Education: Domestic Preparedness and Weapons of Mass Destruction (WMD REALITI)

Four levels of WMD-REALITI (based on the prerequisite competency requirements):

- Level 1: Basic CBRN Identification and Analysis
- Level 2: Effects of CBRN Materials
- Level 3: Structure of CBRN Materials
- Level 4: Advanced Characterization of Unknown Substances

Johns Hopkins Engineering offers homeland security courses that address the following issues:

- Cryptography and information security
- Medical sensors and devices
- Biochemical sensors
- Sensors and sensor systems
- Principles of enterprise security and privacy
- Public key infrastructure and managing e-security

Johns Hopkins University

Part-time graduate certificate program in homeland security systems

Dr. Sam Seymour
11100 Johns Hopkins Rd.
Laurel, MD 20723-6099
Tel.: (443) 778-5711
Email: *sam.seymour@jhuapl.edu*

continued

University/Organization	Type of Program	Contact Information	Background Descriptions of Program
			• Embedded computer systems • Vulnerabilities, intrusions, and protection Mechanisms • WWW security • Network security • Cryptology • Radioactive waste management • Hazardous waste management • Environmental biotechnology • Introduction to systems engineering • Information systems security • Homeland security systems
Joint Interagency Training Center-West (JITC-West), previously known as the National Interagency Civil-Military Institute (NICI)	Continuing education coursework	LTC Bonnie Gosney Director JITC-West P.O. Box 80128 San Diego, CA 92138-0128 Tel.: 805-782-6700 *gosneyb@nici.org*	Tuition-free accredited courses for those in: emergency management, homeland security and defense, U.S. military, nonprofit organizations, public health and safety, fire departments, public utilities, law enforcement, hospitals, and drug prevention. • Consequence management/terrorism • Crisis communications • Agro-terrorism • International borders • Deep-water ports • Homeland security familiarization • Full-spectrum integrated vulnerability assessment

Kaplan College	Terrorism and national security management certificate (online)	Daniel McBride, Senior Faculty and Program Developer Terrorism and National Security Management Kaplan College 6409 Congress Ave. Boca Raton, FL 33487 Email: *mcbrided@adelphia.net.* Charles Lynn, Director of Public Relations Kaplan College On-Line 6409 Congress Ave. Boca Raton, FL 33487 Tel.: (866) 523-3473 ext 7190 Fax: 800-879-0806 Email: *clynn@kaplancollege.edu* *www.kaplancollege.edu*	The Terrorism and National Security Management Certificate program requires a minimum of 36 quarter credit hours. Courses include: • Introduction to the Criminal Justice System • Criminology • White-Collar Crime • Terrorism Today • Investigating Terrorism • World Conflict • Organized Crime
Lamar Institute of Technology (LIT)	Certificate programs and an associate of applied science degree in homeland security	Jim Doane Director of Homeland Security P.O. Box 10043 Beaumont, TX 77710 Tel.: 409-880-2106 Fax: (409) 880-2106 Email: *doanej@lit-mail.lamar.edu*	The Lamar Institute of Technology and the American Institute for Homeland Defense (AIHD) have developed 68 homeland security continuing education courses that provide state-of-the-art training leading to the following six homeland security certificates: • Understanding and Combating Terrorism • Investigating, Preventing, and Surviving Terrorism for Law Enforcement • Homeland Security Intelligence Operations for Law Enforcement

continued

University/Organization	Type of Program	Contact Information	Background Descriptions of Program
			• Weapons of Mass Destruction: Anticipation, Preparation, and Prevention for Law Enforcement, First Responders, and Medical Personnel • Emergency Management • General Certificate in Homeland Security These subject areas are also covered within the coursework required for the associate degree.
Louisiana State University (LSU)	Continuing education and executive training	Jim Fernandez Provost Academic Affairs 146 Thomas Boyd Baton Rouge, LA 70803 Tel.: (225) 578 8863 Email: *jfernan@lsu.edu* *http://www.lsu.edu/ncsrt/*	The Antiterrorism Assistance Program (ATAP) provides international delegations training in anti-terrorism subjects under a cooperative agreement with the U.S. Department of State Bureau of Diplomatic Security. To date, LSU and its subgrantee, New Mexico Institute of Mining and Technology (NMT), have trained 81 countries that have been identified as "in need" of specialized training by the Bureau of Diplomatic Security. Courses include: • Advanced Crisis Response Team Training • Crisis Response Team Training • Critical Incident Management • Explosive Incident Countermeasures • Hostage Negotiations • Obtaining Public Support for Police in a Terrorist Environment

| Massachusetts Institute of Technology (MIT) | Homeland and global security website (central repository of research and education opportunities in homeland security at MIT) | Daniel Hastings
Professor of Aeronautics and Astronautics
Co-Director, Engineering Systems Division
E40-251, MIT
Cambridge, MA 02139
Tel.: (617) 253-0906
Fax: (617) 258-7733
Email: *hastings@mit.edu* | • Officer Survival
• Post-Blast Investigation
• Rural Border Patrol Operations
• Senior Crisis Management
• Tactical Commanders Course

Coursework examples:

• Network and Computer Security
• Integrating Information Systems
• Global Information Systems
• The Airline Industry
• Science, Technology, and Public Policy
• Contending Theories of International Relations
• Organization Theory and the Military
• Ethnicity and Race in World Politics
• U.S. Military Power
• Ethnic and National Identity
• Out of Ground Zero: Catastrophe and Memory
• American Science: Ethical Conflicts and Political Choices
• Political Change in South Asia
• Technology in a Dangerous World
• Reading Seminar in Humanities, Science, and Technology
• Energy, Environment, and Global Politics |

continued

University/Organization	Type of Program	Contact Information	Background Descriptions of Program
Michigan State University, Global Community Security Institute	Certificate in homeland security studies (online) offered by the School of Criminal Justice	Phillip D. Schertzing, Ph.D. Director, MSU Global Community Security Institute 1407 S. Harrison, 346 Nisbet Bldg. East Lansing MI 48823 Tel.: (517) 432-3156 Email: *schertzi@msu.edu*	Courses for the Certificate include: • Foundations of Homeland Security • Issues in Terrorism • Public-Private Partnerships in Emergency Preparedness and Homeland Security Certificates in information security, food security, and related areas are currently being developed.
Ohio State University, National Academic Consortium for Homeland Security	Coursework within the international studies major	International Studies Ohio State University 3086 Derby Hall 154 North Oval Mall Columbus, OH 43210-1347 Tel.: (614) 292-9657	Available coursework in homeland security: • Development and Control of WMD • Terror and Terrorism
National Defense University, including • Industrial College of the Armed Forces • National War College • School for National Security Executive Education	Coursework on homeland security through NDU's Institute for Homeland Security Studies; also a counterterrorism certificate	Deborrah Morris 300 5th Ave Bldg. 62 Fort McNair, DC 20319 Tel.: (202) 685 2128 Email: *nduregistrar@ndu.edu*	National War College course topics include: • asymmetric warfare • terrorism • biological weapons • cyber weapons • missile defense • law enforcement • intelligence • current initiatives

| National Graduate School | Certificate program in homeland security | School for National Security Executive Education (SNEE) offers a 30-week counterterrorism certificate, including:

• Terrorism
• Counterterrorism
• National Security and Civil-Military Relations
• U.S. Foreign Policy in an Age of Terrorism
• America's War on Terrorism
• Foundations and Issues of Homeland Security
• Organizing Homeland Defense

The program is designed for managers, administrators, officers, and those responsible for developing and implementing strategies and procedures in homeland security.

Courses include:

• Homeland Security Principles and Practice
• Contemporary Issues in Homeland Security
• Integrated Studies in Homeland Security and Quality Systems Management
• Homeland Security Field Project
• Management | Dr. Robert Gee
President
The National Graduate School
186 Jones Rd.
Falmouth, MA 02540
Tel.: 1-800-838-2580
Email: *rgee@ngs.edu*

Diane Bonavist
Assistant to V.P. of Enrollment
The National Graduate School
Tel.: 1-800-838-2580
Email: *dbonavist@ngs.edu* |

continued

University/Organization	Type of Program	Contact Information	Background Descriptions of Program
National University	Master of science in homeland security and safety engineering (online)	Dr. Shekar Viswanathan Academic and Administrative Headquarters National University 11255 North Torrey Pines Rd. La Jolla, CA 92037-1011 Tel.: (858) 642-8000 Email: *sviswana@nu.edu*	Required courses include: • Statistics for Safety and Security Professionals • Introduction to Safety Engineering • Chemical Process Safety Engineering • Managing Information Security • Fire and Explosion Engineering • Science of Explosives and Biological Threat Materials • Planning and Response for Terrorism • Capstone course in Safety and Security Engineering
Naval Postgraduate School, Center for Homeland Defense and Security	Master of arts degree in national security, with specialization in homeland defense	Paul Stockton Associate Professor of National Security Affairs Associate Provost for Development Naval Postgraduate School 1 University Circle Monterey, CA 93943-5001 Tel.: (831) 656 3038 Email: *pstockton@nps.navy.mil*	Coursework for the master's includes a thesis and 52 credit hours of courses such as: • Asymmetric Conflict and Homeland Security • Information Technology Management for Homeland Security • Critical Infrastructure: Vulnerability Analysis and Protection • Intelligence for Homeland Security: Organizational and Policy Challenges • Strategic Planning and Budgeting for Homeland Security • Civil/Military Relations for Homeland Security • Special Topics: Agroterrorism, WMD

Purdue University, Homeland Security Institute	In the process of investigating the development of an "Area of Specialization in Homeland Security" that would be available to B.S., M.S., and Ph.D. students and augment their major degree.	Alok Chaturvedi Director Purdue Homeland Security Institute Krannert School of Management Purdue University West Lafayette, IN 47907 Tel.: (765) 494-9048 Email: *alok@purdue.edu*	Course requirements under development.
San Diego State University	Interdisciplinary Master's degree in homeland security	Dr. Dolores A. Wozniak Dean College of Health and Human Services San Diego State University San Diego, CA 92182-4124 Tel.: (619)594-6516 Fax: (619)594-7103 Email: *dwozniak@mail.sdsu.edu* *http://www-rohan.sdsu.edu/dept/chhs*	Offered as an interdisciplinary degree with the following colleges participating: College of Health and Human Services; College of Sciences; Professional Studies and Fine Arts; College of Arts and Letters. The student will be required to take 30 units overall, including a thesis or special project. The student will also be required to take at least one 3-unit course as listed below in each of the following areas: public health, Sciences, communication and political science/ISCOR. College of Health and Human Services, Public Health: • Epidemiology • Epidemiology of Infectious Diseases • Bioterrorism Preparedness and Response

continued

62

University/Organization	Type of Program	Contact Information	Background Descriptions of Program
			Professional Studies and Fine Arts, Communication/Criminal Justice Administration: • Persuasion • Seminar in Administration of Justice • Seminar in Health Communication College of Sciences, Geological Sciences: • Photogeology and Remote Sensing • Sensor Networks • Collaborative Visualization College of Arts and Letters, Political Science/ISCOR: • Seminar in Politics • Seminar in General Comparative Political Systems • Seminar in Homeland Security
Syracuse University	National security and counterterrorism law certificate Program (College of Law); master's in public administration with concentration in	(contact for both programs) William C. Banks Institute for National Security and Counterterrorism (INSCT) School of Public Administration	Required courses for the law certificate include: • National Security Law OR Perspectives on Terrorism • National Security and Counterterrorism Research Center (team research projects)

63

international and
national security
policy (Department
of Public Administration)

Electives include such topics as civil rights, bioethics, international criminal law, mass communications, constitutional criminal procedure, etc.

Courses available for the concentration in international and national security policy include

- U.S. National Security and Foreign Policy
- Asymmetrical War
- American Strategic Practice in a Turbulent Century
- International Security
- Wars of Choice: Presidents and the Decision to Go to War
- Defense Challenges in a New Century
- Global Issues: Drugs, Crime, and Terrorism

University of Connecticut

Executive education

Roy E. Pietro
Executive Director
Workforce Development Institute
College of Continuing Studies
Citigroup Education Center
200 Constitution Plaza
Hartford, CT 06103
Tel.: (860) 566-1195
Email: *roy.pietro@uconn.edu*

In addition to a substantial first responder training effort, the Homeland Security Education Center provides leadership education via eight programs, typically one day to two weeks in duration.

These courses include:

- Certificate in Government Leadership
- Management Development Institute
- Quality of Leadership

continued

University/Organization	Type of Program	Contact Information	Background Descriptions of Program
		Homeland Security Education Center Rowland Government Center 55 West Main St. Waterbury, CT 06702 Tel.: (203) 805-6446 Fax: (203) 805-6631 Email: *roy.pietro@po.state.ct.us*	• Strategic Leadership • Effective Communications • Changing Role of a Leader • Living Leadership • Leadership in Action
University of Denver	Certificate in homeland security offered through the Graduate School of International Studies	David Goldfischer Program Director Graduate School of International Studies 2201 S. Gaylord St. Denver, CO 80208 Tel: (303) 871-2564 Email: *dgoldfis@du.edu*	Students with bachelor degrees will receive a certificate in homeland security upon completion of seven courses and an internship. The following courses are required: • International Terrorism • American Government and Policymaking • Homeland Security: Introduction • Homeland Security, Civil Society, and Human Rights Students must take at least one of the following: • Homeland Security: Prevention and Mitigation • Homeland Security: Response and Recovery • Intelligence and National Security Policy

Additional courses offered include:

- Regulatory Policy, Public Choice, and Administrative Law
- Homeland Security and the Law
- Nuclear, Biological, and Chemical Threats

This part-time certificate program is designed for personnel working in the areas of public safety, security management, and law enforcement; executives in corporations responsible for overseeing in-house security programs; and information technology professionals.

Required courses:

- Introduction to Industrial Security
- Physical Security
- Security Management
- Introduction to Information Security (CyberSecurity)

Electives:

- Criminal Law
- Terrorism
- Domestic Terrorism and Hate Crimes
- Criminal Profiling
- Forensic Psychology
- Special Topics: Chemical, Biological, and Radiological Threats

University of Massachusetts, Lowell

Certificate program in security management and homeland security (on campus and online)

Joseph Lipchitz
Professor
Chair of History Department
University of Massachusetts, Lowell
One University Ave.
Lowell MA 01854-2881
Tel.: (978) 934 4144
Email: joseph_lipchitz@uml.edu

continued

University/Organization	Type of Program	Contact Information	Background Descriptions of Program
University of New Haven	Master of science in national security; master of science in national security and public safety; graduate certificate in national security	Dr. Thomas A. Johnson, School of Public Safety and Professional Studies University of New Haven 300 Orange Ave. West Haven, CT Tel.: (203) 932-7260 Fax: (916) 962-2921 Email: *tjohnson@newhaven.edu*	The programs are offered at both the University of New Haven and Sandia National Laboratories in Livermore, CA. Required core courses include: • National Security Programs Architecture and Mission • NSP Personnel Security Programs • National Security Charter, Legal Issues, and Executive Orders • Securing National Security Information Systems • National Security Internship I or Research Project I Electives include courses in situational evaluation, threat modeling, cost modeling and contract administration, policy analysis, studies of the intelligence and counterintelligence communities, safeguards, and countermeasures.
University of Southern California	Master of science and graduate certificate in system, safety, and security (online)	Randolph Hall, Ph.D. Co-Director for Homeland Security Center Senior Associate Dean for Research University of Southern California	Degree and certificate are offered by the Industrial and Systems Engineering Department and are targeted to professionals in the aerospace industry. Required core courses for both the master's and certificate include:

continued

	School of Engineering University Park 3650 McClintock Ave., Room 200 Los Angeles, CA 90089-1450 Tel.: (213) 740-4885 Email: *rwhall@usc.edu* *http://engineering.usc.edu/homeland_security/*	• Engineering Management of Government Funded Programs • Financial and Economic Decision Making • Value and Decision Theory • Public-Sector Economics • Risk Analysis
	C.L. Max Nikias, Ph.D Dean and Kaprielian Professor of Engineering Tel.: (213) 740-7832 Email: *engrdean@usc.edu*	Electives include courses in the areas of cybersecurity, environmental security, critical infrastructure, policy and planning, and structural safety.
Worcester Polytechnic Institute	Certificate in homeland security	The certificate is composed of the following six courses:
	Elliot Field Director of Sales 100 Institute d. Worcester, MA 01609-2280 Tel.: (508) 831-6789 Email: *efield@wpi.edu*	• Impact Analysis and Structural Crashworthiness • Structural Design for Physical Security • Explosion Protection • Structural Design for Fire Conditions • Construction Failures: Analysis and Lessons • Risk Management